A House, Undone

A House, Undone

For Peter Pereira, and 30+ years of shared poems. with love—

T. Clear

T. Clear

MoonPath Press
Albiso Award Series

Poetry
ISBN 978-1-936657-61-2

Cover art: *Ex Voto 2*, printing ink on paper, 11" x 8 1/2", by Iskra Johnson. Used with permission of the artist. iskrafineart.com

Author photo: Peggy Barnett
peggybarnett.com

Book design: Tonya Namura using Adobe Garamond Pro

MoonPath Press is dedicated to publishing the finest poets living in the U.S. Pacific Northwest.

MoonPath Press
PO Box 445
Tillamook, OR 97141

MoonPathPress@gmail.com

http://MoonPathPress.com

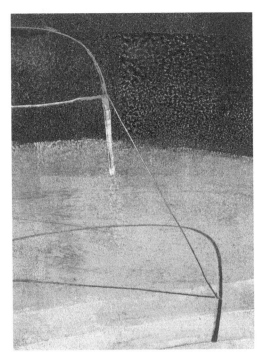

In memory, Mark Benchley Anderson
1956-2003

Contents

An Aggregate of Twigs

A House,
Undone

Deadbolt

"Was it yesterday I stretched out the thin
bones of my innocence?"

—Theodore Roethke

Life Sentence

I live in a house of scant beginnings,
of rupture and leakage,

splinter and rot. A wire
dangles to nowhere, something

cut mid-sentence, a thought
that will never complete itself.

A house of raveling sweaters
and unpainted stairwells.

Crack in the glass, hemless curtain,
the last bit of aluminum foil

flattened and folded one more time.
Awaiting the phone call, the letter,

a knock at the window,
crow at the door—

here lie all my unfinished cadenzas,
my abrupted couplets.

Home Sweet—

We went forth, we insulated,
we sawed, added. We lumbered
and lingered, designed and deliberated.
Amortized for thirty years.

We plumbed, we electrified.
We routed out the rats.
Dropped cloth, slapped paint,
fastened-down, bolted-to.

Hammered-in. Evened-up.
We set the screws.
We enclosed. We finished-off.
Put on final coats.

We subtracted, recalculated.
We yanked-up planks.
We shaved, splintered, stripped.
Switched-off, hacked-out, pried-up.

Disassembled. Returned for refund
while it burned & blistered, slipped
from the foundation. It leaked,
dripped, as ants feasted in the eaves.

It was peeling-off, leaning-to, protruding.
Glass cracked, shingles lofted, hinges unhinged.
We pulled up our boots, we dug-in,
buttoned-up-to-our-chins. Hunkered,

tossed the anchor, inflated the parachute,
hoarded blank checks and spare tires.
Notarized the Declaration of Insurance.
Swept up, polished-off, *to-the-last-drop*.

Fasted. Prayed.
Got down on our knees.
It would always be home.
Nothing else mattered.

Safekeeping

Days without sun pile up
like dirty socks, the sky a muddy wash.
I want to whisper the crocus
back under the muck,
furl each petal, every slender leaf.
It's too soon, I say, *too cold*.

There was a time I wouldn't go to sleep
until every doll or button-eyed bear
was covered for the night.
Short a blanket, an errant sock
made do. I kept my toys snug
all through the winter months.

Come April, I set them out
beneath the apple tree
where petals drifted down
like remnants of snow, pale sun
returned at last, the sky
scrubbed-clean of mudsock grey.

Peter-the-Dog

His set-in-cement canines
could rupture a thigh.
Face like a pickaxe, peg-legged,
he was a muscled runt
who braced to dodge a stone
tossed at his solitary eye.
A growl like crushed gravel.
Victor tethered him on a chain,
steel-toed boots aimed at the ribs.
We crouched behind a hedge,
listened for a few kind words.

Death fetched the wife and her lace hankies,
her handouts of sugar cubes.
Victor-the-Widower mastered bingo,
nailed off a hallway of bedrooms.
Lived the remainder of his life
hunkered in front of an open oven.

And Peter-the-Dog?
Our own local bestiary entombed him in the cellar
beneath a soiled spade, a boot tufted with fur.

Subdivision

As soon as fir planks climbed a stairway
to the second floor, we moved in,

the gang of us out to play after supper
where our voices rang in the rafters

and we strutted between measured studs,
between rooms yet to be defined.

The forest so recent, we breathed it in
with every uncarpeted step. Every nailed board

as young as our own green limbs.
What universe would set up house here,

behind sheet-rocked walls and a locked door?
Squatting rights expired

as soon as parents called us home to bed,
our deed of ownership imprinted

in the timber's grain, everywhere
we touched, everything.

The Nest

On a low branch of a plum tree—
the boy next-door claimed it,

bragged blue eggs all that June day.
Didn't matter in whose yard

the grove of four plum trees grew,
but it wasn't his. My sisters argued,

staked the border with a row of sticks,
sat vigil until bedtime.

The next morning, Mom
walked out in early sunlight,

something not right, some
tensile shift in the air, perhaps—

And then it was all slash
and snapped branch, all disbelief

and leaf askew and hard green plums
in a scatter on the ground.

And then a wing,
or a silent fragment of wing.

And then another.
How many ways to ravage?

A beak beaten into dirt.
The blue shard-edges of shell.

She made a sling of her apron,
lifted the feathered scraps into gingham.

Buried it behind the swingset
at the edge of the woods.

Come August, she put-up a winter's worth
of dusky plums in syrup, dozens of quart jars

lining shelves in the basement dark,
each sugared pit an eye at the heart of the flesh.

Colony

A splash of gasoline, a match,
my brother poking it with a shovel.

I was too young to have an opinion,
yet knew it was wrong.

Even if the haystack pile of it
grew each day more troubling

beside the swingset, beside the prim
lines of carrots in the garden.

A gush of smoke, that acrid
stink of their dying—and then finished.

I trailed back later
to check the fuming wreckage,

discovered a highway of ants
crawling deeper into the woods.

Thousands, some lumbering eggs
on their backs, a frantic jumble

punctuated with tiny sticks, bits of stem.
I didn't yet know the word *frenzy*.

Didn't know this was the way
things happened: fire, destruction, exodus.

Vigil

Hours at the kitchen table with my father
and my uneaten peas, and him settled
into the evening *Times*, maybe a pipe.

He had the rest of his life to wait.
I had until a looming bedtime—
which lingered into centuries

as the evening dwindled.
He mentioned the starving children
on the postcard from my aunt, the nun.

I told him I'd send every last pea
in an envelope to Africa, give up
half my dinner every night

for my release. He told me
no more backtalk. I swallowed
forkfuls of whole peas to bypass

the smear of them in my mouth.
Calculated peas-per-swallow,
considered my diminishing glass of milk.

Clank of fork on the ceramic plate.
My sisters' laughter from another room.
Outside, robins spiraled their twilight song

up from birch tops. I could hear a game
of tag in the next yard, planes above
going anywhere away from where I sat.

There was no rescue.
I suffered them down; dashed out
to the remnant of a summer night.

Limits of Spectacle Lake

When the sun had slipped behind the hills
I said, *Let's go back*. Forget this business
of lures and lines and casting so far
the eye could hardly follow the thread
out to snag a rainbow's lip. Afraid
we'd lose our way and soon our boat
would spin and sink. There we'd sit
eye to eye with a million fish.

When I was eight, I caught my limit.
But not before my father turned the boat
to shore and let out one last line for luck.
I held that rod for all the hope left
reeling in the depths. I pulled
trout from tangled, churning light
slipping underhand.

I don't know who was more the spectacle—
the lake, me, or my father guiding the pole
between my unbelieving hands. Somehow
he trusted in the end of all filtering light.
When he died the next winter,
I remembered six fish
laid out on a plank.

Eye to eye with the dead, in the wake
of the boat, I learned the limits,
the last ripple of life in a dying fish.

Silence in Winter

When there was no longer someone
to play the fiddle, my mother
banished it to the basement
beside idle saws and hammers,
in the company of the ticking furnace
and flannel-wrapped rosin.

*

A man named Andy sang Ave Maria
at my father's funeral, kept in time
by the flat-footed organist.
My mother and all seven of us kids
in the front row at St. Anthony's;
my brother, the oldest, called home
from the Air Force.

*

Neighbors bought the piano, rolled it
across yards on planks laid end to end.
No more jigs and reels.
No more *Bug in a Rug*.

*

Winter evenings stretched across a starless horizon
as we penciled homework at the kitchen table.
My mother with a drink in one hand,
on the rocks. The light dulled, as if
half the lamps had been unplugged.

Door *i*

I dreamed a door that wouldn't close—
loose hinges, slippery lock, misaligned.
Backed up against it, wedged a foot to hold it.
Slammed shut, it slivered open
and always something on the other side
to keep out, or let in.

The last door by which my father left;
a slice of apple pie, the fork
where it had dropped
when the artery at his neck
collapsed. Who did my mother call?
Because she didn't drive, no time,
no permission with seven kids.

I like to say that he wore his hat
and a wool tweed overcoat
the last time I saw him,
but who can trust a nine-year-old's memory?
Not my older sisters, each with her own version.
And who shut the door
once he was gone?
Asleep that night, was it the first time
I imagined a faulty bolt?
No: a deadbolt
I wouldn't let engage.

Door *ii*

A way in, a way out.
Sometimes the way through
in spite of the deadbolt.

There was the time the glass shattered
as the wife was thrown against it.
The infant, still so much a part of her flesh—
shielded in her arms.
The soft swirl of hair on his fontanel
like the smallest of feathers.
A miracle of no blood.

Then the door was plywood
nailed in a hurry to keep out
the winter rain. Until the next day
when the glassman came
with his single pane
and putty, like a band-aid
that never quite covers the gash.

What the door kept in
the wife kept secret.

Outside the door,
a border of thorns,
black-spotted roses
that died back
below their graft
to bloom a sorry petal
minus scent.

From the street:
an ordinary door.
A glass panel.
Someone behind a curtain.

Our Lady of Flotsam

       O she who keeps watch
over the rubbished, the odd shoe, the cracked
crockery flung in rage, the zipper pull,
chunks of airborne, waveborne Styrofoam.
Vigilant mother-of-pearl, of cockle & scallop.
All ruin, all glorious sand-glinted treasure
is welcomed into her o-holy-arms.

       Tides strew a briny indulgence
at her feet. She makes incarnate the shred,
the bit, the fragment. Grants goodness
to the twist-top, the peach pit, the tangled line.
Gull beaks beseech her name, crab hulls
praise the stones which tumble upon her strand:
forever and ever an ocean of discard.

The End of Childhood

I kept a rabbit,
black and white in a hutch
under the apple tree,

more feral than pet
in constant quiver. I'd grasp it
by the nape, fasten a tiny harness

over neck and shoulder.
Let it out on a leash
so it could feel some grass

under its paws. Held back
its lunge to escape with a rope.
Until I found its plank and wire

home gashed open, tufts of fur
marking a path to the woods.
I surrendered to a darkness

that prevailed under hemlocks and firs,
a god without a name, baring tooth and nail.

Abscission

1.

Where are they now, the trees
of my childhood ascensions,
the elbow-scrapers, the chin-grazers,
all the thin-limbed windy branches
that held my skinny bones
aloft, and only barely—
those nest-cradlers and eggshell tippers,
fledglings on edge—and I was one of them—
my self-ejection in the hormonal rush of thirteen.

2.

The fall to earth set my brain atilt;
what girl played in the woods
with a bulky pad wedged between her legs?
My abandoned forest gave way
to a cul-de-sac. Instead of a branch
I grew a breast nub, and another.
My mother insisted on lipstick
but my pale mouth desired only song
sung from the highest branch of the highest maple.

3.

Decades.
My own eggs now cracked and bled.
The old trees from whose limbered branches
I hung upside down
surveying the canopy
from downside-up—
or balanced high in dwindling treetops
as I sang the evening out
in a voice not yet broken—
day is done, gone the sun—
they are lost now to all

who never knew their windy sway,
their autumn leaf-heave, their winter osteology.
Set to burning in smoke-hooded pyres.
Never to know the headboard of a bed,
nor a bedside table for a book
or the paper bound within.
No stump remains to mark the years.

Bootstraps

Pull yourself up, they say.
As if all you needed
was an inch of elevation.

But you can't pull
if you don't have boots,
or the straps are missing.
Doesn't matter how high-up you pull
if the sole has worn through,
if the sock is more hole
than thread.

No good if you trip
and laces drag like reins on a runaway horse.

Your life is that runaway horse,
bolted clear away
through a fallen-down fence
and you're so far behind
you can't even see
the beginning of the road
the horse ran off on.

How did you get here, on your bloodied knees?
When did it all become so impossible?

You hear it again:
pull yourself up by your bootstraps,
as if the answer to every problem
was as simple as listening
to this broken record.

Bad Thumb

This is the finger crushed
between doors, age six
before mass, offered up
to the god of no ice: thankless and bruised.

The stub scrumbling in loam,
awkward flinger of carrot seeds,
a thousand to the ounce.
This is the pit end of the shovel,

digit no one claims
from the bin of lost appendages,
stump with the spatulate nail, ugly in polish,
begging for a blunt clip.

Never the soft lamb, the silky tip.
Sandpapered, abraded of tissue.
Whorl of a tornado, spiral
of no-good, a print-on-record.

This is the thumb that wouldn't get a job.
The thumb that finally lowered the shade,
pulled the pin, cocked the hammer.
The thumb that raised itself

roadside, no apologies. Hopped
into a truck, vanished.

Breakdown

When the dryer failed
I hung a week's washing
in sun above snow—
skidded out in flimsy shoes
on an icy crust that crackled
with every slippered step.

Gloves meant clumsy clipping.
And nothing dry in the unpinning—
each sock, each frayed sleeve
stiff as a bone sucked clean.
No bend in a trouser-knee.
No easy flutter among bedsheets.

Every stitch and thread
held tight to its ice—
no romance, no feathered comfort.
Broken, and broke:
ice brittled in every empty pocket;
thawed, finally, in its own dull time.

Cloud Trouble

Here is summer's sailcloth blue stretched from hem to hem;
and there, a gauze apron, a sheer skirt

afloat
        below indigo.

How thinly stitched this perfect sky seems—
liable to tear itself loose and leave me
with the wet grey of winter wool
just when I thought all my cotton clouds
were pressed and folded into tidy cumulus stacks.

Something wants to rip this silk into rag-edged scraps,
let loose a hailstorm of fret and frayed bindings.
Unravel the rick-rack ridges of updraft, the thready strands.

I'd just as soon put down my pressure-foot and reinforce
each flimsy seam. No more falling apart in the wash
of rain, in the fluff-and-tumble of wind.

I'll have this blue calm ceiling sewed-up tight
before the next gale blows it apart—
the funnel-cloud zippered down,
the blizzard needled, the cyclone
gathered into orderly ruffles.
A doubled knot, back-stitched,
a dress of clean-edged days.

Fault Lines

"Love. The black hook. The spear singing
through the mind."

—Louise Erdrich

Protocol

A knock on the door, 2am.
Two men and a woman,
black, white, chaplain, police.
Clipboards. Bible.
Their faces dread the apologies
for which they bear no blame.
Strangers, who knew before me
that my husband departed
the scene zipped into a sack.
I will not recall their names,
or know if, roused by duty,
they left a sleeping household
much like mine; the only difference
being that moment's hesitation
in the turn of the wheel,
foot on the brake.

Body Parts

They wouldn't let me
at the body.
Said,
We need a few days.
We'll let you know.

Meanwhile,
they scooped out his brain
and weighed it.
Weighed his heart,
his liver.
Made note of his last meal,
the alcohol-swirl
in his veins.
His "Funk Blast"
t-shirt, scissored
down the middle
to release him
to the scalpel.

When finished with the scale,
the ruler,
all was piled back
into the slit-open cavity
that was my husband.
Even the brain,
packed back
into a fractured skull.

When the funeral director called
I said
Show me the hands.
The hands and forearms.
No stitchery of jaw and lip,

no thick paste of stage makeup.
I wanted to claim the blood-
truth of what was left:
sinew, cartilage,
all the pooled bruises.

Even so,
I reached beneath the shroud
to cradle his head—
what god of mercy
granted me
a fistful of hair
and nothing else?

Containing Grief

I'd suffer an umbral shadow
in a lunar eclipse, my aura rimmed
with a blistering bruise.
In cotton bales I'd lumber
under kilo after kilo, mouth dry
as a foolscap-quad of paper sheets.
In hat sizes, twenty gallon.
On the Glasgow Coma Scale:
complete gibberish.

If measurable, then disposable,
like a broken bed or a newspaper.
Burnable like a cord of wood,
expendable as wattage. Frittered away
like minutes. Walked away from:
the bad job. Downed by the pint.
Shed, subtracted from, divided by.
But not this rank tonnage
spilling, spilling.

Litigation

The plaintiff wants my house,
its accumulation of equity.

The plaintiff wants my wallet,
my $50 savings bond,

my nine-year-old Mazda.
The plaintiff says, *My life is ruined.*

I say, *My husband died.*
The plaintiff cites *broken jaw,*

pelvis, right little finger.
I cite *transection of the spinal cord.*

My children say nothing
and a dead man says nothing.

I slept while bones splintered, sinews severed.
My children slept, until I shook them

awake to this unhinging.
When metals collide

the fact of a single day fractures
into a junkyard of blame,

a scorecard of misery
no almighty dollar can repair.

The Hit

He said, *I can take care of this for you.*
Word was he'd done time.
Ran the chopper shop down the street,
came in for the daily special,
left a $20 tip on a $6 tab.

Swaggered into the kitchen
like he owned me, eyes blue
as the hottest part of a flame.
Never mind the *Hells Angels*
tattooed across his back.

Or that he was 26, I was 47.
That his girlfriend was named
Jasmine. Told me he loved
his mom. Told me,
I can take care of this for you.

Can I say that for a fraction of a thought
I considered it? The way the mind
can rev-up a scenario and all its possibilities
in less than a single intake of breath?
That this lapsed-Catholic girl was willing

to let slip every last law
to make this nightmare disappear?

Possession

From a web of dreamless sleep
I wake before dawn
to an alarm of crows,

open the door
to their frantic swerving
top of the pine

where a lone eagle
clutches the highest branch,
unnerved by attack.

I doubt an eagle cares
about ownership of a tree,
but nineteen years of possession

of a house beneath these boughs
has convinced me that the crows own the pine
outright, no back payments,

no outstanding debt to nature.
No court will remand it, nor judgment
tear it from their claws.

Not even the eagle, who eventually
lifts his wings in a sauntering swoop,
disappears into the grey veil.

The Poem Who Drank Too Much

Too many nights in the margins of gin
and he blanked out, rhyme and reason

shaken, his marriage
on the rocks. The wife

wanted out of the couplet,
threatened a stanza break.

He buried his dissonance in rum,
jiggered his diction, but—

there was trouble in parody.

You used to have such a beautiful simile, the wife said.
You're always feeding me the same line, he said.

We don't have syntax anymore, she said.
I'm averse to abstinence, he said.

She left him for a novel.

He mixed his metaphors with vodka.
His tone grew flat, his liver stressed.

No longer the stirring ode,
the poem who drank too much

nursed a swollen foot, became a hack,
had his license revoked for writing

under the influence. Lived out his sentence
as a cliché scribbled on a brown paper sack.

Table

Not an island, not an isthmus
or a spit. Not a peninsula.
The kitchen table is a land mass
untethered to the vinyl floor,
prone to slippage if it weren't
for the lumbered-mass of it.
Built waist high, meant for larger tools
than a whisk, a spatula, a cooling rack.
Meant for a saw, hammer, drill.
Raw-edged planks, no fussy trim.
Wrestled up the basement steps
and put into service
after a decade of disuse.
Long enough to lay out a dead man
on a cloth, if there was need.
Or a woman.
Long enough to lay out 30 pies.

Flag

If my kitchen had a flag
it would be this tattersall towel,
c. 1983, stolen from a hotel cupboard
in France. We were barely married
and already the groom, a thief.

This towel, that blotted blood
when a knife slipped, wiped a pan,
rumpled under a chin to catch a drool.
That plumed with flame, dripped
a charred corner, wrung from the sink.

Trimmed and frayed,
it outlived the groom
turned husband turned dead.
For the life of me
I couldn't throw it away.

Perpetually stained,
it hung from the clothesline,
when the dryer ceased to tumble,
froze when left out overnight:
unflappable pennant.

Encumbrance

Every month I make payment
on a debt brought about by two men
both dead as dogs ditched at the roadside.
Whose only meeting was an accident,
a head-on spinout, one injured,
one deceased. My husband,
one drink over the legal limit.
I was liable, default owner
of everything by way of marriage.
All the well-meaning friends
who insisted it wouldn't happen:
No one sues a widow with kids.

I made him an offer:
divide up what's left,
cut a check for his portion.
He wanted more, demanded
millions I didn't have.

Thirteen attorneys told me *yes* or *no,*
maybe, try this, sell that.
Move to Texas, Alaska, Florida.
Spend everything but on nothing
durable. Take vacations
on your equity, eat out often.
I lost the taste of value.
Lost my business,
lost my sons to grief. Too late,

Dear Husband:
too late to fix the brakes, stop
at one beer, decline that last shot.
Too late to come home after work.

To Willie Winston, plaintiff with the broken bones:
were you glad you healed?
You got your cash,
I got the bill.
And then karma did you in:
what little heart you possessed
called it quits.

Letters to a Dead Husband

1.
Mark, I have to tell you:
the starlings returned
to nest in the eaves
where you neglected repair.
You never loved them,
yet last year waited to roust
the messy twig and mud jumble
until each fledgling soared
clear of gutter and roof.
Grumbling, glad to be done,
this was your unexpected gift
and I never thanked you.

Soon summer will spread its wing
over this unfinished house
where porches and railings
await the carpenter's hammer and nail.
Our children—nearly men—
will desire to roam the city all night,
and I'll let them go
one feather at a time,
always holding back
and then releasing, alone now
instructing in the mechanics of flight.

2.
I'm righting the house you left askew,
untipping the groundwork you laid,
fault lines that began to slip

after your exit. How many days
did you dig, muscled deep in a slurried trench
to pour concrete set rigid with rebar?

Something unsteady underground
that no one could see, months skidding
forward into hairline cracks

that grew by the millimeter,
grew by the year, the dollar.
All the edges of life buckled.

Alarms blared. I changed the locks.
Changed them again. Bolted windows
but this breakup would not relent

and now it's come to this.
How far down must I go
to set this house straight?

3.
Enough. Take your feathers
dead or alive and flutter into oblivion.
I'm done with the fractured wing,
the punctured lung, severed spine.
I will not weigh your soul
and account for all its cherished works.
Though your nest lies ruptured
and broken at my feet, all my remedies
are used up, finished, expired.
Mud no more, dear downy love.
Burn the twigs, the riffraff rags.
Let the cats loose.
Fetch the axe.
I'm cutting down the tree.

After Long Waiting

I surrendered the fabric bits of you
to the 99¢ bin at Goodwill—
t-shirts, socks, mismatched or not.
No rush to vacate the closet.
What could have taken an afternoon
eased into months, this slow letting-out
of your seams, my unraveling.

I imagined meeting a stranger
wearing the blue wool sweater
I wrapped for you that last Christmas—
what would I say to him?
What words could possibly make sense?

Your shoes were last to go.
As if somehow you might return
and step back into your life.
I kept them paired beside the bed
for the silent comfort they offered
while I slept on both sides of the mattress.

Yet I suspect a single boot remains
under the basement workbench—
the left foot, laces undone.

It's been ten years.
You're late.

Repository of the Lost

I went there once, with bare toes,
one ungloved hand, hoping for reunion.
By myself, thinking I could find
a man I'd lost, that he'd be there too
hopping about on one booted foot.

I wore a single earring.
Found a wing, a ski, a chopstick.
One stiletto heel. Saw a one-eyed boy
looking for his twin. Saw an ear.

There were plenty of socks
in striped heaps, in rumpled hills of wool.
But of course, not a one matched.
And mittens, unclipped.
Not so many shoes, fewer knitting needles
and a single lung, bled out.

It felt like death, all those severed
attachments. Like divorce.
Like the last place on earth I'd look
and still not find the mate.

O my glove, my lost love,
my soft pink slipper, my handcuff—
how will you know I've come
to take you home? Tell me, how
will I find you in this oblivion?

I will send you a vessel containing nothing—

A pocket, no coins.
Scraped plate, a glass
with no residue of wine.

Emptied uterus.
Sleepless bed,
a pillow, no feathers.

House without walls,
a clear-cut forest,
vacant sky.

Not a cloud,
not a star.
I will erase

every word from this poem
before I send it to you
in a blank envelope.

Don't look for it
in your mailbox—
there's nothing there.

And what will be left
to hold in your hands
when all the world

is turned on its side
and every last thing
spilled out?

Denouement

What if this is the end of possibilities?
What if this is all we have?

Here is the last cure, the final documents,
every signature blasted into stone.

No more ancient bones begetting
a more ancient man. No deeper,

no farther, no faster. This universe
that measures 93 billion light years

from end to end contains everything
we can ever know. Nothing smaller

than a quark, the last new specimen
on a slide, frozen behind glass.

So tell me: where would you go
if all your hopes could only travel backwards?

Departing the House of My Former Life

Once I close the door, hear the click
of the latch, there's no going back.
I may run circles around it, peer

into each window as long as desired,
but entry is impossible. The single key is,
from this day forward, forever lost.

Best to gather the few remaining flowers
before the garden lapses into ruin,
fill my pockets with apples.

Disavow all I've abandoned
inside this lathe and plaster fortress,
every root still clutching a fist of soil.

Better to leave and not return,
not recall the accumulation of broken beds,
the last unshattered cup, the wedding china.

And a rock thrown at a pane makes bad luck.
I'll unpin the solitary dress hung ragged
on the line, yank the numbers

from the siding, check the mailbox.
No curtain wavers; every candle's a stub.
Not a soul to wave me on but my own.

An Aggregate of Twigs

"That's my only defense against this world:
to build a sentence out of it."

—Jim Harrison

When Houses Fall Away

One summer night the floor slipped
quietly westward. Not a jolt
but a motion smooth, the only creaking
in the boards beneath your bed
where you slept, dreamless and still.

For months your house perched on blocks,
the foundation crumbled beyond repair.
Neighbors offered their two cents
while carpenter ants bore into crevices
of damp and silent wood.

The earth's crust shifts and trembles,
civilizations slide away. We build,
we pound and cement our lives
onto rectangular plots of earth.

And without knowing, suddenly we lose
a step. For a moment there is only
the dishes rattling in the sink,
the teetering house falling away.

An Autobiography of Cheese

First, I was milk.
Sucked from my mother's teats
by mechanical lips clamped and groaning
as I swirled into sanitized tubs.
Calves bawled for me.

I shivered in the dark belly of the tanker,
hemmed in by steel. Couldn't stop
my sloshing, my heaving waves in the rumbling din.

Emptied into a vat, I felt my aqueous temperature
inch upwards. Remembered my mother's udder,
my bliss as I hung in the sac—
my sling, my skin cradle
rocking under her ruminant heat.
How brief those hours, how fleeting
our milky youth.

Acidified, the whey drained
until I was only curd: I wasn't half my self.
I was protein and fat,
a salted wheel in a chilled room.
I suffered my own aging.

Microflora ripened me.
Enzymes heightened my tang.
Without a choice I lost
the taste of milk.

Drawn and quartered, my value soared.
I knew I couldn't stay together,
knew my parts would be carried off.
What of me would remain to tell my story?

My plastic shroud is peeled away
and for a few hours
this sweet air is all mine.
My rigor softens.
I've grown a bit of a stink,
but that comes with the price.
The board on which I lie
could be a coffin in another life.

Fox Territory, County Galway

Not my ankle splayed there, stripped
of meat, not my ribcage, my skull
discarded on the bog. Solitary horn.
Most likely an unlucky sheep,
spinal tissue still visible.

Behind me a stone cottage hunkers
in decay, vulnerable to stars.
One black boot, god knows how long.
A steel trap, teeth locked
on decades of rust.

How easy to be this victim:
a simple slip, a collision
of flesh and rock. Rendered
immobile in peat, tucked back beyond
hill after hill. The distance out

measurable only in the fleet foot
of the fox, for whom this day
quite possibly promises abundance.
But not me, not these precise steps
around, away from, abandoning

this boneyard. Not this hand,
this ear, this throat. I press
a relentless path into the wind,
keep watch, go quickly
quickly.

Cheap Motels

They smell you coming.
Like mildew they stick around
for centuries with volunteer bibles
and archaic rates posted
on a hollow-core door
you could kick-in without even trying.
Curtains sigh in a cigarette breeze.
Cheap motels desire disinfectant
and a shower that doesn't drip.
You wish for more bucks.

They love a slob.
Truth is, they love beer cans,
spilled Doritos, No-Pest Strips, runny
toothpaste and dust bunnies.
Truth is, so do you.
You'll settle in like another
broken-backed easy chair,
feet on the sofa, floral upholstery.
In a minute or two you'll snore.
The motel won't hear you.
The cheap ones listen for money,
clink of a dropped nickel.

Trespass

Split in an earthquake, the floor gapes
to expose the underbelly of a house
too many years ruptured.
A sofa untufted, disgorging
upholstery like spume
from a rattled earth. Unswaddled
baby-doll, uncradled. No
soup pot set to simmer,
no coital remnant of sheet
where no bed remains. A shiver
in the pink mold that blooms
on every wall. Nothing
that warms to the living.

Supplication to Our Lady of the Dumpster

O lid of clang & wheels of clatter,
O collector of rubbish & swill, O Holy Mother
of great pickings, of dreck & slop: Hear our prayer.

O saint of litter & scrap, protect us
from the banana peel, the Styrofoam chunk,
from all that defies *reduce/reuse/recycle*.

O divine casting off, O sacred decay!
Hallelujah to the Hefty Ultra-Flex 33 Gallon,
the drawstring, the twist-tie.

Praise to those who dive into the belly
of your dump—the urban foragers, the hungry,
scraping a meal of crust & bone.

Consecrate them, O Queen of rubble
robed in graffiti. Watch over them,
that they may not themselves become waste

to be managed, a cubic yard of flesh
primed for front-loading. Now,
and at the hour of their death.

Steadfast

I yank tangled vines from a hundred years
of Douglas fir soil, knee-deep in ivy
that will cinch an untended tree

in a noose, excrete a glue laced with steel.
When a root surrenders, I careen backwards
into needled loam, more humus than human,

a fragment of the understory. Half my life
I've kept this tree from the chainsaw's snarl,
accepted that any blustery night

could mean death for the both of us,
my bed squarely in the blowdown path.
I'd curse my persistence in a final breath.

Cave

When my sons disappeared into the earth
I stood still on the path and listened
to the bright silence of their absence.

Nothing shook, no bouldered racket
of a hillside collapse. No clapquick
thunder rolled down from the heavens.

No change but their sudden descent
where only a heartbeat ago we'd paused
on the trail for deeper uphill breathing.

I could have forbid their pied piper
desires, stood barricade before the abyss
that lured them into the dark.

Yet in the end, a simple truth:
I let them go, and stayed behind
and stood on that mountainside

for what felt like the rest of my life,
only longer. Time shifted shape,
disassembled the minutes until

every second was a separate agony.
My cut-loose heart went also,
carried off on a spike: heigh-ho.

Of course, they emerged from the scree
mossy-headed, mud-kneed, spilling
their story like a balm into my bones.

And my heart slipped back in, pumping
blood to my blue throat, my lips.
I knew this was practice, the beginning.

Atilt

An old house wants to lean,
as if it's a child slouching
over meatloaf and peas.
Sit up straight, I say to the walls,
The house doesn't listen.
Can you blame it?
A hundred years is a long time
to keep a framework true.
The more it sags,
the more it wrinkles.
But what about those cracks,
like faltering heart lines?

It takes a crew to drill down
21 feet before finding rock
worth digging a tooth into.
They lever it up with creaks and groans
a quarter inch at a time,
every joint an old man of complaints.
Did I just call my house an old man?
Feels like a husband most days
for all its demands, its liabilities.
And if I want it to sit up straight,
well then, goddamnit,
that's what it's gonna do.

Blue

If I say
I'm going to paint my house *goat,*
it doesn't mean I keep a goat in the house
but that I'm going to paint it
a certain grey tone, found on page 57
of *A Dictionary of Color,* ©1930.
Yet that would be a lie
because I already painted it *starch,*
or *daphne,* or maybe *zenith,* hard to tell.

Everything hinges on the light,
how *lagoon* becomes *iceberg,*
and *virgin* sheds innocence to *afterglow*
as a cloud conceals the sun.
Some mornings I awaken to *opal*
and come home to *slag.*
In a drizzle, *king's blue* fades to peasant.
All so slippery.

I want to say that my house is *Aphrodite,*
that it's *Versailles* and *love-in-a-mist,*
But that old *goat* keeps showing up,
stays the winter, lingers into July.
And here I am a year older.

Stealing Cherries

Once, we had a plan
to wait for enough of a moon
to light a thieving path between houses.
We'd need buckets, and a wheelbarrow
to roll away the buckets. Yes—
we wanted all of them.
Not a handful, not a mouthful or pocketful,
but every last ruby-blushed Royal Anne cherry
lighting up the tree that belonged to us
before the sale of house and acre.
When summer afternoons we lazed
beneath laden branches and believed
the world would always contain enough
to feed us cherries without end.

Where did that life go,
or did it even exist
outside the white picket-fenced past?
The tree was long-ago axed
to clear a path to suburbia—
empty buckets.

Shelter

I dwell in a box under the freeway.

I dwell in a hut, a car, a lean-to.

I dwell in a tent, on a sidewalk with rats.

I dwell in a ruined parking garage with no running water.

I dwell in a tenement, a trailer, a studio.

I dwell in a two-bedroom apartment with my family of ten.

I dwell with Old World Charm, with leaded paint.

I dwell in an urban setting.

I dwell in a condo with 2 ½ baths and guest towels.

I dwell with *access to* and *amenities such as*.

I dwell with security and a view.

I dwell in a development, in manufactured housing.

I dwell in a rambler with *room to grow*, with *ready for your imagination*.

I dwell with gates, with covenants for window coverings and paint color.

I dwell with approved shrubbery, a mortgage, and HOA dues.

I dwell with surveillance.

I dwell with a three car garage and three cars, a yacht at the marina.

I dwell with an oceanfront vacation home.

I dwell with privilege as long as I keep up the monthly ransom.

Affordable Housing Is on the Endangered List

1. *Demolition*

Two box-houses will replace this one
three-story, four-square, classic American
architecture: run down, double lot, subdivide.

See the backhoe dig into the kitchen,
the dining room, the living room.
Watch it yank down 115 years of living

in an easy hour, time is money. Watch it
drive right up to the top of the debris
and yank some more: stairway, bedroom, bedroom,

bedroom. See the roof corner tip, then topple
as old-growth fir planks splinter
into a dump truck, engine running.

See ghosts wave farewell from the dust
as they are swept up into the breeze
after ousting. See them float somewhere south.

Each box priced at $1.4 million,
or 360 payments of $5492
after 300k down, at 4.375%.

2. *Notice*

The city has announced that all unauthorized
homeless encampments will be swept
at the end of the week.
Swept, like dirt into a dustpan.
Swept, like litter.
Like garbage.

3. *Outdoor Living*

It's legal to camp if you make reservations
and pay up-front, online, months in advance.
It's legal to camp if your tent features
250-denier polyester-oxford *X-Treme Tent Cloth*.
It's legal to camp if your tent
has an accessory vestibule, a briefcase-
style bag and sidewall pockets for iPads.
It's legal to camp if your tent
is a yurt, or if you call it *glamping*.
It's legal to camp if you put on a costume
and pretend it's the War of 1812.
It's legal to camp if you can park
your Hybrid beside your tent.
It's legal to camp if your stay
is less than 14 days.
It's legal to camp if you don't
chop down a live tree.
It's legal to camp if, at the end
of your 13-day stay, you get in your
2021 Dodge Durango Citadel and drive home
to your $1.4 million dollar house
with remote controlled garage door,
100% recycled-glass kitchen counters,
reclaimed white oak flooring throughout,
locally harvested hemlock beams,
a composting toilet, and a clever
waste-water heat-recovery device
that operates without the use of electricity
or any fuel and is fully sustainable.

4. *NIMBY*

A neighbor knocks on my door
to tell me that a homeless man

has moved-in to the empty lot
at the end of the street.

Says she thought I should know.
Wonders what we can do about it.

I'll bring him a sandwich, I say.
You would do that? she says.

Maybe you could bring him some water, I say.
I couldn't do that, she says.

He's a human, I say.
We need trained professionals, she says.

There are places where he can go, she says.
And where is that? I say.

Downtown, she says.
Where will he put his garbage? she says.

I'll bring him a garbage can, I say.
Who will empty it? she says.

I say, *The only difference between you
and him is that you can pay someone*

to take away your garbage.
The next morning, I watch her

move her trash cans to the curb for pickup.
The lot at the end of the street is empty.

5. *Real Estate*

Three miles away, a homeless encampment
crowds the mudlot between freeway off-ramps.
Blue Tarp is the favored color choice

and security is a two-way zipper.
There's no parking, but it's on the bus line.
There's no electricity, but loads of natural light.

No kitchen, but close to a dumpster.
Yours for a shopping cart and a tent.
Location! Location! Location!

Pilfering

A house wears abandonment like a shroud
draped in spider silk and guano.

I wander the remains, expect collapse
where floorboards sprout a carpet of ferns.

Here, one blue cup forty years emptied of tea.
A drawer of past due bills stirred up

with a spoon, an eggbeater, a butter knife.
I find rosary beads tucked into a damp box,

the tarnished virgin linking a string of fragments
more dust than pearl, absent a crucifix.

I hear a litany across my own lapsed decades,
feel it in my knees as I recite remnants of prayer—

one holy Catholic church
the communion of saints—

I pocket the beads—*bless me father—*
check behind me—*for I have sinned—*

The wind sighs forgiveness as I drive away.

59 Twigs

Pulled from the dryer vent—
an interrupted nest
threaded together with lint.

A blockage.
A stoppage.
My twinge of regret

as scant as a splinter.
I expect the wind
to sweep it away

because it weighs less
than an eggshell.

*

But the next morning
it's still there—crackle-
bundle, fire-starter—

my guilt.
Home wrecker!
Nest wracker!

*

I lay them out to photograph—
long to short
on a spread of white paper

until they are four feet across
and nearly disappear
to woody specks.

A single breath would send them
up in feathers. Is it hubris
to think I could make more

from this aggregate of twigs
than what it never became?

Wintering With Bees

When I'm lost roaming the frozen fields,
let me be small enough to enter a honeyed hive
so that I may fold myself, shoulder to shoulder,
into the sweet company of their cluster.

As winter deepens, we'll huddle ever closer
to the queen, conserving our own
shiver-borne heat to stay alive,
vibrating a low hum deep within

an old tree's trunk. A way to endure
the dark, and a hundred pounds of honey
to sustain us. Come spring the girls
will rustle up a scent of pollen, take flight

to dredge their legs in golden grains.
Will I have grown a black and yellow coat?
And lucent wings to lift me
back into my human self?

Or will I stay to fan the nectar,
content to spend my hours
in trembling dance, pointing the way
to the sugared brew?

Grown Old

You return, weary as mildew
to a door that sags a final hinge,
a slug-trail lit by the moon
through a window's puzzled shard.
Every angle webbed with cocoons.

How long since morning
and your clockless waking?
And where have you been?
No hat, not even a sweater
to soothe your shivered husk.

This is where it ends:
your last measure of repose
on a bed littered with leaves,
starlight for a roof.

This Life

This one, with the wrinkled shirt
and a stuck zipper.
That snores.
This life with a missing tooth.
That makes too little money.

This life with food stamps.
This life with no car,
or a broke-down car.
This life with an empty tank.

This life that trips you and breaks your glasses.
This life that pulls you over.
This life that bills you,
charges interest, bills you again.
This life with a late fee.
This life that forecloses you.

This life that keeps breaking up with you.
This life that won't ever marry you.
This life that divorces you, again.
This life that says *you'll never get it right*.

Yes, this one.
This life that won't let you go.

This life that calls you *cunt, bitch*,
that gets up in your face and says
keep it up you know what I'll do.
This life that drinks too much
and leaves your glass empty.

This life that kills you,
yet in those last few minutes
you'll plead for more of this life
that will walk away
and not turn back.

Notes

"Our Lady of Flotsam" and "Fox Territory, County Galway" were written in the West of Ireland, in a most enchanted place called Carrowholly.

The setting for "Cave" is Tiger Mountain, Issaquah, Washington, where I learned that an entrance to a cave can be so small one can easily pass by and never know the transitory terror of seeing one's children disappear into the earth. It's dedicated to Reilly Anderson and Nelson Anderson.

"When Houses Fall Away" is dedicated to Roy and Chrissie Marshall, neighbors and friends for 34 years. And whose steadied house stands, to this day.

"Stealing Cherries" was written for my sister, Lorraine Clear Barrett.

"Pilfering" is dedicated to Gregg Foreman, my accomplice.

"Limits of Spectacle Lake" is in memory of my father, Walter James Clear, 1918-1966.

Acknowledgements

The author would like to thank the following journals where these poems first appeared, some in earlier versions, or with different titles:

Anti-Heroin Chic: "Our Lady of Flotsam"

Bayou: "Bad Thumb"

Bayou: "Peter-the-Dog", "Bad Thumb"

Cascadia Review: "Limits of Spectacle Lake"

Crab Creek Review: "Body Parts", "Possession", "Flag", "Repository of the Lost", "Letters to a Dead Husband", section 3

Crannog: "Blue"

Iron Horse Literary Review: "Cave"

Passaic/Voluspa: "I will send you a vessel containing nothing—"

Raven Chronicles: "Possession", "Departing the House of My Former Life"

Red Earth Review: "The Poem Who Drank Too Much", "Wintering with Bees"

Slant: "Letters to a Dead Husband", section 1

Slipstream: "Cheap Motels"

Sweet Tree Review: "Life Sentence"

Switched-On Gutenberg: "Cloud Trouble"

Tab Journal: "Grown Old"

Terrain.org: "Abscission"

Thimble Literary Magazine: "Door *i*", "Door *ii*"

Tuesday Poem: "Supplication to Our Lady of the Dumpster"

Urban Spelunker: "When Houses Fall Away"

"Limits of Spectacle Lake" was awarded The William Stafford Award, from Washington Poets Association.

"Body Parts" was nominated for a Pushcart Prize by the editors of *Crab Creek Review*.

"Repository of the Lost" was nominated for the *Independent Best American Poetry Anthology* by the editors of *Crab Creek Review*.

Gratitude

A generous measure of thanks....

To my Easy Speak poetry family, past and present, whose
warm-hearted welcome was a lifeline when I'd nearly given
up on poetry, and whose continuing friendship is the
very definition of community, at its best; especially Peggy
Barnett, Kris Beaver, Christine Clark, Mary Crane, Donna
James, Ra'anan David, Mark Johnson, Ted McMahon, Erika
Michael, Lynn Miller, Peter Munro, Jed Myers, Paul Nelson,
Rosanne Olson, Philip Patton, Alex Smith and Bonnie
Wolkenstein.

To my sons: Reilly Anderson, for persevering with kindness,
wit, and understanding; and Nelson Anderson, who lent
a patient and insightful ear to many early drafts of poems
when he was a teenager.

To my sister, Mary Clear-Padilla, a devoted audience
member at countless poetry readings spanning four decades.

To Cezanne Hardy, whose seed-pod stitchery and
cryptographic emails never fail to ignite my sense of wonder
and further the belief that this world contains infinite yet-
to-be-explored depths.

In memoriam, to two of the finest people I've known, Tom
and Carol Porter. If you still have my pizza pan, I would like
it back.

This record of appreciation wouldn't be complete without
mentioning the mentorship of Nelson Bentley (1918-
1990), poet and University of Washington professor, under
whose tutelage I learned that one could be a poet and
also live a perfectly ordinary life. (Although "ordinary"

is a slippery word, open to myriad interpretations.) His generous spirit, his sense of humor, and his inclusive community of poets profoundly shaped how my next forty years of "poeting" would play out. To honor his legacy after his death, I launched a workshop group, which evolved into the South Grand Poets, from which sprang the humble beginnings of Floating Bridge Press, which continues to publish Washington State poets today. His "never put a battleship into a poem willy-nilly" has been my guiding principle, ensuring that every word in a poem better damn well be there for a reason.

Finally, heartfelt gratitude to John Albiso for creating this award to honor the poetry of his wife, MoonPath Press author Sally Albiso, who passed away in 2019; to Priscilla Long, judge for the 2021 Sally Albiso Poetry Book Award; to Lana Hechtman Ayers, MoonPath Press Managing Editor and Publisher; and to Tonya Namura, book designer.

About the Author

T. Clear was born sixth of seven children, into a noisy, crowded, and loving family. The too-small red house that housed the family of nine bumped up against Pacific Northwest second-growth woodlands, open fields and orchards. Her earliest memories are of wandering among Douglas firs and alders, legs skirted in bracken ferns, ever-wary of stinging nettles. With her five sisters (and one brother) she harvested hazelnuts and apples, boysenberries and rhubarb, the promise of pie luring all back into the kitchen to gather each evening for supper. From that gentle life her first poems emerged, a practice that grew to become as organic as lifting a decaying log to reveal the treasures beneath—a translucent salamander, a clutch of glistening snail eggs.

As the only of her siblings to complete a four-year college degree, she studied verse writing at the University of Washington, and continued there in the Graduate Writing Program, where she studied with Nelson Bentley, David Wagoner, William Matthews, and the Welsh poet Leslie Norris. She was fortunate to take a week-long intensive workshop with Richard Hugo a year before his death.

Her first poems were published in 1975, in the newsprint publication *Yakima*, and since then have appeared in many magazines and anthologies.

A lifelong Seattle resident, she has two grown sons and works in Human Resources.

CPSIA information can be obtained
at www.ICGtesting.com
Printed in the USA
FSHW011637281021